Money Matters:

The Get It Done in 1 Minute Workbook

www.BiggerThanYourBlock.com

They say the journey of a thousand miles begins with one step. Consider this one step to further your journey.

Table of Contents

This workbook was created from questions people have asked during conversations and workshops over the last three years.

Each module begins with a short explanation of the topic, is followed by a question, has the answer to the question, and, if appropriate, closes with a worksheet to help you follow the steps in the answer. Have a question that's not answered in this workbook? Email it to Questions@BiggerThanYourBlock.com and your question may be answered in the Money Management in 1 Minute Video series or even the next workbook!

Getting Started

You bought this workbook because you want to make some changes in your financial outlook. Changing your wallet is going to have a lot to do with changing your mind. In this workbook, we'll take a look at how you think about everything from credit scores and net worth to relationships. If you want to get different results, you're going to have to do things differently.

The first step to get your finances in order is figuring out how much money you bring in, how much you spend on taxes, how much you are saving, and how much you are investing. The worksheet on the next page will help you see the bigger picture of your finances.

Take a moment and fill out as many areas as you can. Don't worry if there are areas that are empty, that means that those are areas that need to be worked on. So, let's get started.

Getting Started Worksheet

Income
How much money do you earn per year? _____

Taxes
How much money do you pay in taxes every year? _____

Banking
In the last year how much, if any, money did you pay in bank fees?
     Account fees _____
     Overdraft fees _____

Savings (short term)
Do you have an account for emergency money?   YES   NO
What type of account is the emergency money in? Savings   Money Market   CD
What is the interest rate for this account? _____
How much money is in that account? _____

Savings (long term)
What long term goals are you saving for?
     #1 _____
     #2 _____
     #3 _____

What type of account is this in?   Savings   Money Market   CD   Investment
What is the interest rate for this account? _____
How much money is in that account? _____

Investments
Do you have an investment account?   YES   NO
Do you have an Individual Retirement Account?   YES   NO
Do you have a 401k account?   YES   NO

Liabilities
What is the total amount of debt you owe? Include student loans, credit cards, mortgages, auto loans, debts to friends/family. _____

Did you leave some spaces blank? No worries! We'll work through figuring out everything together.

Savings

Savings falls into two general categories: short term (in the next five years) and long term (longer than ten years). We will all have emergencies come up, and having just $500 available for emergencies may be the difference between paying bills and going into debt. Short term money needs to be available at a moment's notice to pay for car repairs, tickets, and other emergencies. Make sure to put your short term money in a savings account or money market account that has a high yield. A savings account is an account that a credit union or traditional bank offers. Savings interest rates tend to be low earning you little money in interest every month. Money Market Accounts are accounts offered at a credit union or traditional bank that restrict your access to funds by limiting the number of times you may make deposits and withdrawals, however offers you higher interest rates. Check www.BankRate.com to compare some accounts. Knowing what's available will help you know when you've found a great interest rate. Long term money can be put into more risky and less liquid accounts because you won't need the money for a long while; think about certificates of deposit and retirement accounts.

Savings vehicles also fall into a few broad categories:

Savings Vehicles	Short Term Appropriate	Long Term Appropriate
Savings Account	●	
Savings Bonds		●
Money Market Account	●	
Mutual Fund Account		●
Retirement Account		●

Reader question:
What is a strategic way to tackle debt? For example if you're late on your Sallie Mae [student loan] payments and credit card bills which one should you tackle first? Can you really pay what you can afford when it comes to having an account in collections and what is the best way to negotiate that?

Getting *into* debt took time and getting *out* of debt will take time.

Student loans and credit cards are serious business. Getting back on track with both are equally important. Which one to begin sending your money to depends on how late each account is, what the interest rate is, and how flexible each company is willing to be with repayment. There is no one-answer-fits-all solution. Using the Debt

Worksheet on page 6 will help you list your debts and figure out which ones should be top priority.

Government and private student loans will usually try to work with you by offering deferments and forbearances to help you manage your budget before you are late on payments. Once you are already late, you might be in a different boat. Contact your student loan provider and be honest about your situation. They will likely ask you to provide evidence of your inability to pay such as pay stubs. They may be able to reduce your monthly loan payments or defer them until later.

Having a credit account in collections is a horse of a different color. Sometimes when you are late on a bill, the company may forward your account to a collection agency. Usually collection agencies will work out a payment plan that will fit into your budget, however be careful: interest is usually accruing while you pay off the debt. Alternatively, the collection agency may tell you that you can pay a fraction of what you owe in order to pay off the debt; don't believe it until you see it in writing. There have been many cases of collection companies saying one thing and doing another. If you want to pay off the debt, contact the original company and work out a payment plan.

If the account is so late that it has been wiped off the books of the original company, you will have to deal with the collection company. Here are a few helpful tips about any business transaction:

- Make sure to get everything in writing.
- Request that the collection company provide you a letter once debt is paid off.
- Keep copies of all correspondence for at least 7 years.
- Mail all payments with a copy of the original agreement.
- Once debt is paid off, check all 3 credit reporting agencies (Equifax, Transunion, Experian) to make sure that the account says "paid".

In short, deciding whether to pay off student loans or credit cards is a decision that will be based on many factors. If at all possible, I would suggest one of two strategies. The first is to pay a little on each to get back on track and the other is to figure out which has the highest interest rate and put as much money as you can toward that debt until it's paid off. I think paying the minimum amount due on all bills and putting extra debt payments towards the debt with the highest interest rate is the quickest way to get back on track. By paying the debt with the highest interest rate off first, you will save money on interest payments, cross off one debt at a time off your list, and be able to use the money that you were paying the highest interest debt with to pay the next highest interest debt and continue the plan until all your debt is paid off.

Remember that as long as you are late on *any* debt payments, your credit score is being hurt. Be honest with the companies, be honest with yourself, and be patient. Create a plan to pay off debt and stick to it.

Debt Worksheet

Name of Debt	Contact Info	Total Debt	Interest Rate	Notes
Example: Olivarria Credit Card	(800) 474-0403	$3,500	18%	Call on Tuesday to set up a repayment plan.

Start by making the minimum payment due, on time, to each bill.

Which debt payment has the highest interest rate?

_____

How much extra money can you put towards this debt every month?
$_____

Which debt has the second highest interest rate?

_____

Once the first debt is paid off, how much extra money will you be able to put towards paying off the second highest debt? $_____

FICO Scores

You can get a free credit report from www.AnnualCreditReport.com once a year for free. You will not be able to see your FICO scores. The most common type of credit scoring system is the FICO score created by the Fair Isaac Corporation. There are three major credit reporting agencies: Equifax, Transunion, and Experian. You can get all three credit reports with FICO scores from www.MyFICO.com for $48. It is important to check all 3 credit reporting agency's file on you because each may have different information. Make sure that all the information is correct. Companies can put anything on your report. It is up to you to make sure that the information is correct. If you find errors, you can update info and dispute debts online, by phone, or in writing. The whole process takes only a few minutes. Check your credit reports often.

Reader Question:
What is a credit score and why is it important?

Let's make sure we're all starting from the same point. The FICO system determines a score for each individual borrower between 300 and 850. There are three credit reporting agencies: Experian, TransUnion, and Equifax. Each credit reporting agency receives information from companies that it contracts with. That means that each agency may have different information in your file. Lenders know this. Smaller companies may contract with only one agency; larger companies may contract with all three. For example, when you apply for a store credit card, that company may contract with Transunion. The company will pull your credit report from TransUnion only and based on that credit report alone, they will decide whether to extend credit to you. Now let's say you're looking to buy a home. The mortgage lender will have a system that contracts with *all three* credit reporting agencies. All three of your scores will be pulled and the middle one will usually be used. The lender is aware that file discrepancies occur, so if you have a 750 at Experian, a 700 at TransUnion, and a 800 at Equifax, the 750 will be used to decide whether to extend credit to you. Ensuring that your credit files are correct is paramount.

Monitor your credit reports at least once a year for accuracy. Disputing things on your credit report is as easy as logging in to the online site and clicking the button that says dispute. Choose the drop down item that describes why this information is incorrect and type a little reason in the box. The credit reporting company will have to go back to the original creditor to make sure information is correct. Once you are sure that all your information is correct, you want to make sure to keep your credit score as high as possible.

There are four main ways to raise your credit score:
- Monitor your files for accuracy.
- Pay down your debt ratio.
- Pay bills on time.
- Manage different types of credit (revolving accounts, installment loans, etc.) responsibly.

Credit scores are created by complex algorithms taking into account several different pieces of information and computing a numerical value of how much of a risk it thinks you are. The five most important pieces of information that help create your credit score are: timely bill payments, managing different types of credit, length of credit history, new credit applications, and debt ratio.

What your credit limits are in comparison to how much credit you've used is what's called your debt ratio. Lenders want to see that you have access to credit that you're not using to feel comfortable lending you money. Paying bills on time is also very important. If a bill is due on the 20th, don't wait until the 20th to pay it. Make sure that there is ample time for the company to receive and post your payment. A late payment can torpedo your credit score pretty quickly. Lenders like to see that you have a long and varied history with credit. The longer you have managed credit, the more responsible they hope you will be. New credit applications, sometimes called hard inquiries, are important to limit. Every time you try to get credit, with a few exceptions, a note is made in your credit report. Limit your new credit applications to things you really can't live without. Lastly, lenders want to see you handle different types of credit including revolving loans (credit cards) as well as installment loans (car payments) responsibly.

Credit Report and Score Worksheet

Agency	Score	Info Correct?	Notes
Equifax P O BOX 740256 Atlanta, GA 30374 General: 800-797-6801 www.Equifax.com			
Dispute:			
Dispute:			
TransUnion PO Box 2000 Chester, PA 19022 888-259-6845 www.TransUnion.com			
Dispute:			
Dispute:			
Experian PO Box 9556 Allen TX 75013 888-397-3742 www.Experian.com			
Dispute:			
Dispute:			

Retirement Accounts

There are two basic types of retirement accounts: Individual Retirement Account (IRA) and job based accounts termed 401k for private sector jobs and 403b for public sector (non-profit) jobs. Each of these accounts offers two options: Traditional/regular or Roth. The difference between Traditional and Roth is when you pay taxes.

With Traditional accounts you are taxed on the money you put into the account when you take it out of the account. You can take a yearly tax deduction for any contributions that you make into the account. Most people are in a higher tax bracket while working and in a lower tax bracket in retirement, so people that use a traditional account are banking on the expectation that money in the account will be taken out after they have stopped working and they owe less money in taxes every year. Penalties and taxes will be put on any withdrawals taken out before you are 59 ½ years old.

The Roth account is not taxed when you take the money out because you are taxed on the money before you put the money in the account. That means when you are in retirement, you can take out money without having to pay any taxes on that money. The other benefit of a Roth account is this, you can take out the principal at any time without penalty. Only the interest, if taken out before you are 59 ½ will be taxed and assessed penalties.

Individual Retirement Account (IRA) Could be Traditional or Roth
- You are the only one adding money to your account.
- Only $5,000 may be contributed in 2008 for those younger than 60.
- Possible penalties for taking money out before 59 ½ .

Employer Sponsored 401k/ 403b
- All contributions are before taxes. Instead of paying the government, you are paying yourself.
- Many times employers will contribute matching money. It's free, so take it!
- Up to $15,500 may be contributed in 2008.
- Penalties for taking money out before 59 ½ .

Reader Question:

I don't make that much money, but I want to start saving and investing for my future. As of now, I would only be able to afford to invest $50 a month in a mutual fund. One financial planner told me that is not enough money and I would never see growth. Is she right? Is there a minimum number that we should be investing each month? And if there is, what should the rest of us do who can't afford it?

First off, I would like to apologize to you for having to work with such a negative person. All financial advisors, money managers, etc. should be encouraging people to begin where they can. Once some good saving and investing patters are established, one can work toward increasing the amounts over time to reach their goals. Everyone should be saving whatever they can a month. Assuming you're 25 even saving $1 a day will net you $132,585 by the time you're 65 in a Roth IRA.

I used an online calculator to find out how much $50 a month can add up to. Let's assume that you are 25 and want to start withdrawing money from your account at 65.. If you start socking away $50 a month now and increase your contributions over time to the max allowable you may be able to have $1,873,463 in a Roth IRA! In a taxable account that figure might change to $1,025,565. The best part? This calculator assumes you only contribute $215,000. Where does the rest of the money com from? The magic of compound interest!

The magic number for saving "enough" for retirement is to try and save 12% of your income. If your job offers a 401k or 403b, take advantage. Most employers that offer a 401k/403b also offer a match. That means that your job will contribute money into your retirement account for you, for free. Companies used to provide pensions, since they don't do that too much anymore many companies offer matches. The money vests, becomes available for your use, after a set amount of time. They don't want you to contribute $1000, they put in $200, and you walk off the job the next day and take their money with them. If you decide to leave your position with the company DO NOT take the money out of the retirement account. What you want to do is roll it over to your new retirement account.

If you withdraw money from a retirement account for any reason it may trigger a tax bill, check with your tax professionals for specific instances when it will not, however if you have the institution with the money send the money to the next institution that you want it to go to a tax bill will not be created. It doesn't matter if you have the institution mail you a check and you mail a check to the new institution. To the IRS you took a distribution - end of story.

In the end, saving something is always better than saving nothing. As you get used to putting away money into a retirement savings vehicle, you can increase the amount to achieve the goal that you have set for yourself. Don't let others dissuade you. Only you know what your goals are and how you can reach those goals within your budget.

So, how much money do you need to be able to retire comfortably? No one knows for sure. It depends on the type of lifestyle you want to lead in retirement and what debts you'll have to pay. Use the Mutual Fund Worksheet on the next page to begin thinking about how much money you have, and how much money you would like to have, in retirement.

Mutual Fund Worksheet for Employee Sponsored Plans

1. My employer sponsors a retirement plan. (Ex: 401k or 403b)   YES   NO

2. The company that manages that plan for my company is

_____.

(Ex: Ariel Mutual Funds, Prudential, Vanguard, etc.)

3. I have money taken out of my check every pay period that goes directly to this employee sponsored retirement plan.   YES   NO

4. I want to retire at age _____.

____ I plan to spend my time at home, relaxing.

____ I plan to spend my time traveling.

____ I plan to spend my time working on projects.

____ I plan to continue working part-time.

5. I want to have $ _____ by the time I retire.

6. I have to save $_____ a month, at _____ % interest rate in order to achieve this goal.

There are several online retirement calculators; each one uses a different formula. Computing how much money you need is a complex question, however to get a ballpark figure calculators are wonderful. One that might be helpful is http://moneycentral.msn.com/retire/planner.aspx Play with different contribution amounts to get a better idea of what the outcomes might look like.

Congratulations! You've just taken the first steps toward securing your future! After completing this worksheet you may want to talk to an account representative about where your money is going every month and what it's doing.

You can measure your plan against other plans at http://www.brightscope.com/

Mutual Fund Worksheet for Individual Investment Accounts

1. I save on my own for retirement through an IRA.   YES   NO

2. My account is: ROTH   TRADITIONAL

3. The company that manages my IRA is

_____.

(Ex: Ariel Mutual Funds, Prudential, Vanguard, etc.)

4. I have money taken out of my check or checking/savings account every month that goes directly to this plan.   YES   NO

5. I want to retire at age _____.

____ I plan to spend my time at home, relaxing.

____ I plan to spend my time traveling.

____ I plan to spend my time working on projects.

____ I plan to continue working part-time.

6. I want to have $ _____ by the time I retire.

7. I have to save $_____ a month, at _____ % interest rate in order to achieve this goal.

There are several online retirement calculators; each one uses a different formula. Computing how much money you need is a complex question, however to get a ballpark figure calculators are wonderful. One that might be helpful is http://moneycentral.msn.com/retire/planner.aspx Play with different contribution amounts to get a better idea of what the outcomes might look like.

Congratulations! You've just taken the first steps toward securing your future! After completing this worksheet you may want to talk to an account representative about where your money is going every month and what it's doing.

You can measure your plan against other plans at http://www.brightscope.com/

Stocks, Bonds, and Mutual Funds, Oh My!

Owning a stock means that you own a little bit of whatever company's stock you hold.

Owning a bond means that you have lent money to whatever company holds the bond.

Owning a mutual fund means that you own a group of stocks, bonds, cash, or mix of all of the above.

As a general rule: stocks are risky and bonds are safe. Younger investors tend to have a mutual fund that owns more stocks because investors want more risk to hopefully end up with more reward. Older investors tend to have a mutual fund that owns more bonds because they don't want to risk losing too much money closer to when they will need it.

Reader Question:

I understand that I should start saving for retirement, but I don't know how to open an account and I can only save like $50 a month. What should I do?

1. Decide how much you can contribute every month.
2. Figure out when you would like to retire to get a sense of how risky you can be in choosing a retirement account. 10 years? 20 years? 35 years?
3. Think about how much risk you can handle; you have to be able to sleep at night.
4. Find a company that offers retirement accounts (Roth or Traditional IRAs or your employer's 401k/403b) by researching online and deciding which one fits your risk level.
5. Contact the company to get an investment packet and application.
6. Fill out the 3 page application, attach a voided check, and mail everything in to the company.

For example, the reader can only contribute $50 a month so she needs to find a company that allows someone to open an account with no money as long as she allows the company to transfer $50 from her checking account into her retirement account once a month. Two companies that open accounts for as low as $50 a month are Ariel Investments (www.arielinvestments.com) and T. Rowe Price (www.TRowePrice.com). They both offer several different mutual funds, so make sure that you are comfortable with the fund you choose, but don't stress out about it. Studies have shown that though there are funds that perform very well, and there are funds that perform poorly, most funds are somewhere in the middle. A more important thing to consider is how much the expense ratio is.

The expense ratio is the percentage of the fund's money that the fund company earns for managing the fund. If you can get an expense ratio under 1% that's great. The closer the fund ratio is to 0.0% the better.

Depending on how much time you have before you retire, you may want to have a more safe or more risky bunch of stocks. Usually, the longer you have until you'll need the money the more risk you can take. If you have more questions, please find a fee only investment banker to ask. The banker will require a flat fee to speak with her, however the cost is well worth it for some solid, unbiased advice.

Only you know how much risk will make you check the mutual fund pages every day and how much will allow you to sleep at night. Seriously consider how you might feel if you woke up and realized that 10% of your retirement savings was gone. Big rewards usually mean big risks.

The easiest, and most challenging, way to find a retirement account is by looking online. Another good way to get an idea of what's available is to read Mutual Fund Magazine, Kiplinger's Magazine, or Money Magazine. I found mine by seeing an ad that mentioned being slow and steady when saving for retirement. I went to the website, read a bit about them, and chose a no-load account that had little risk. I wanted to start slow to get my feet wet.

I chose a Roth account because I figured that I would rather miss a tax break now to be able to pull my money out tax free when I needed it. Since I work for myself, I didn't have the option of opening a 401k/403b account.

I sent off for an investment packet that arrived about a week later. I made sure that I could live with their investment philosophy of slow and steady, checked online to see how long the company had been in business, took a look at the history of the fund I chose in comparison with other funds in the same group, and made sure that I would be able to access my money quickly when I wanted it.

After I was satisfied with the account I chose, I filled out the application, attached a voided check, and waited for a letter to make sure my application was received. I have been with the company for about seven years and I'm pleased with the fund's performance. I haven't made oodles of money, however it is quite satisfying to check my online account and see that I've made a few hundred dollars a month for not doing anything.

If you are thinking about opening a retirement account use the Retirement Account Comparison Worksheet on the next page. Keep in mind that previous fund performance does not guarantee future performance. Investing in the stock market is risky.

If you already have a retirement account, use the Retirement Account Allocation Worksheet on page sixteen to begin thinking about your retirement account options.

<u>TIP</u>: choosing a no load account will ensure that you get to keep as much of your money as possible.

Retirement Account Comparison Worksheet

Retirement Account Name	Company Contact Information	No load?	Expense Ratio	1 Year Earnings	5 Year Earnings

You can find fund performances on each company's website. To get an overview of mutual funds offered, Yahoo! has a good tool. Visit http://finance.yahoo.com/funds.

Retirement Account Allocation Worksheet

My investment account (401k, IRA, 403b) invests in the stock market.   YES NO

I am _____ years old.

I would like to retire at age _____, so I have _____ years to reach my retirement goals.

If you have a longer time to reach your goals, you can be more aggressive. If you have a shorter time to reach your retirement goals, you need to be less aggressive. Also, consider what you're comfortable with. Generally, the more money you have invested in stocks the more aggrieve your portfolio is.

You can find the information below by looking at the prospectus that the investment company mailed you, by calling customer service and giving them your account number, or by looking at your account online.

My investment account allocation is as follows:

_____ % Stocks

_____ % Bonds

_____ % Cash

I am _____ to see how aggressive my asset allocation is.

I feel _____ to see this information on paper.

I would like my asset allocation to be _____.

Respecting Yourself Financially

Here is my 1 minute suggestion boiled down to 1 second – Don't Trust It! This is in regards to anything that is mailed to your home offering you credit that you did not ask for. Why do you think the company is offering you credit? Because they want to see you happy? No, because they think that you have a good chance of getting caught in their credit trap. That's right, I said it, "trap". Companies make money when you don't pay your bill off every month. Would you trust someone you don't know showing up at your doorstep offering cash for a loan? Of course not. Instead of looking at the new credit offer in the mail as a windfall, look at it for what it is – a financial trap to keep you in debt. Respect yourself by being responsible with your money.

Reader Question:

I am thinking about having my boyfriend move in with me and I have heard about different ways to pay the bills such as separate accounts and joint accounts. What do you think is the best way to approach paying bills?

The first question I'd like to ask is why he is moving in with you? Does he have his own apartment? Is he capable of paying his bills on time? What's his credit score? Did he… wait, wait, I digress. The short answer is this: I suggest you both keep separate accounts and open a joint account to pay for the joint bills.

Ladies and gentlemen, listen up.

If things go well you'll want a separate account to pay for the things that might be special to you and have nothing to do with the money needed for the bills. If things don't go so well you'll want to have some money in case he clears out the account and runs off. Seriously, when deciding how much to contribute to the joint account the usual advice is to go for equality of intention instead of equality of dollars. Put an equal percentage of your pay into the joint account to cover the bills. Keep the rest of your money in your account. For example, if you bring in $2,000 per month after taxes and he brings in $1,500 per month after taxes, and you each decide to contribute 50% of your income to cover the bills, you would be contributing $1,000 per month while he would contribute $750 per month. If one of you makes more than the other, and you both contribute an equal amount in the joint account, one of you will have more spare money than the other which might cause problems. In this example, while the woman would put $1,000 and have another $1,000 for her personal expenses, if he put an equal amount of money which in this case would be $1,000, he would only be left with $500.

The best way to respect the relationship is to respect yourself. Talk about money before it becomes and issue. You might be surprised to find out that he has been saving for retirement since he got his first job at the fast food spot or that he has spent every dollar that he ever earned, and some that he borrowed. Come up with a clear plan for paying bills for the home as well as personal bills. Think his personal credit cards are none of your business? If he has to choose paying his credit card bill or kicking in his half of the light bill, do you think he would have a problem with having you put his half up until he can get it together? Would you feel bothered by his asking you to chip in his part? Talk about these things early and often. The more the both of you can get on the same page about habits and expectations, the better.

Cohabitating is serious business.

Free Credit Reports

Getting your credit score from all three credit reporting bureaus can be as easy as 1, 2, 3! You can even get it for free. The government enacted Fair and Accurate Credit Transactions Act allowing each person to have access to their personal credit report for free once a year. Annual Credit Report (www.annualcreditreport.com) is the only site that provides access to all three credit reports for free once a year. You will not be able to view the scores, however you can make sure the information is correct and up to date. Don't be fooled by other sites offering you a free credit report. It is usually a lure to get you to buy ongoing credit monitoring services for a monthly fee.

Reader Question

Nowadays what is considered a "good" score for applying for loans, mortgages, apartments, credit cards etc? Is it the same for all of them or are each looking for something different?

That's a very good question. Too many times I hear folks talking about how they have "bad" credit without really understanding:

1) That they have 3 credit scores from each of the major credit reporting bureaus.
2) That each score may be different.
3) That each organization has it's own idea of what is acceptable to extend credit.

Loans
The acceptable credit score for loans varies because the lower the credit score, the higher the interest rate. You can usually find someone to give you a loan regardless of how low your FICO score is because though you are risky, they will make some money off of the loan due to the ridiculously high (sometimes 25%!) interest rate. Always know what your credit score range is and shop around for interest rates. Different companies will offer you different interest rates. Take your time and walk away from a sales representative that tries to pressure you into signing the contract immediately.

Mortgages
Home loans are a little different. A year ago, you could get a home loan with a 620 middle FICO however due to the mortgage debacle most lenders want you to have at least a 700 middle FICO score now. The higher your credit scores, the lower your rate. If you are looking for purchase a home it is imperative that you know your scores going in so you can negotiate for a better rate.

Apartments

This is a whole different animal because of the deposit required and the usual request that the renter make at least 3 times the rent a month before taxes. All three of these pieces can be leveraged to get the apartment that you want.

Credit Cards

There are many different types of credit cards and different credit score requirements for each one. Folks with credit scores over 720 usually don't have too much trouble getting credit cards. Those with credit scores lower than 650 may apply for secured cards, but watch out because many of those cards come with high interest rates, annual fees, and application fees. If a credit card company asks you to pay an application fee, run for the hills! Some of these companies will charge you $50 to apply, an annual fee of $75, and give you a limit of $300. That means when your card arrives in the mail with a limit of $300 only $174 is available.

Another important thing to remember is debt ratio. The debt ratio is calculated by dividing the amount of credit that you have used by the amount that has been extended to you. For example, if you have a card with a limit of $1000 and you have a $750 balance, then you would divide 750 by 1000 to get .75. Your utilization ratio would be 75%. Most companies want you to have a utilization ratio under 30%. This shows that you are using credit wisely.

Remember: it's best to take out credit when you don't need it because when you do, they will tell you that you are a risk. Prepare for a rainy day folks. Prepare for a rainy day.

Thanks Joe Budden! (Decide to Succeed)

I was listening to a Joe Budden tape when I heard something that made me heart stop. He said something like, "there are 3 kinds of people: those who saw what happened, those who don't know what happened, and those that make things happen". This is exactly how I feel about personal finance. Some of us see others get money. Some of us don't know how folks get money. Some of us are the ones getting money. Which one are you?

Reader Question
I'm graduating from high school this year and I'm not sure what I'm gonna do after that. My teacher is trying to get me to apply to college, but I'm not sure I wanna do that. I wanna get a fly car, house, etc., but I don't know how to get it.

First off, I'm glad that you are thinking about the future. Too many of us aren't thinking a month ahead let alone a year ahead. Now, the answer all depends on you. Deciding what you want to do is a long, time consuming, decision. I would like you to pick up Think and Grow Rich: A Black Choice by Dennis Kimbro. The book gives you a wonderful outline for earning wealth.

I teach money management skills to elementary, middle, high, and college students and I hear this question quite a lot. We all want the good things in life, but few of us have a plan to earn those things. Do we think that Opportunity is going to knock on your door one day while you're playing Wii and talking on the phone? Of course not, we have to go out and earn everything we get in life. There are 4 easy steps to make sure you get everything you want out of life: decide what you want, make a plan, don't let others dissuade you, and go get it!

Decide what you want

There is a difference between a dream and a goal. A dream is something that we wish we had; something that we wake up from and face reality. Many of us have dreams of being rich, but what does that mean? How much money is rich? Your goal must be specific and measurable or how will you know when you reach it?

Make a plan

Now that you have a goal, it's time to turn it into a plan. Your plan must be SMART. Specific, measurable, attainable, realistic, and timely. Plot out the steps logically. Crawl before you walk.

Don't let anyone talk you out of your goals

There will be naysayers. Don't let them distract you from your goal. The Chinese have a saying, "the man who believes it can't be done should not interrupt the man doing it".

Go get it!

The last part of these four steps is the most difficult. Many of us have goals, made plans, shared them with others, and then faltered at the last step. This is the part where the work comes in. There is no way to achieve your goals except hard work.

It's really that simple. Decide what it is you want to do, make a plan, don't let others talk you out of it, and go get it.

Go get your dreams.

Net worth

Many of us think about our financial worth in terms of how much money we make a year. This can be misleading. I think we all know people that make $90,000 and spend $100,000. They have all the nice things, but are constantly worrying about credit card debt, car payments, and keeping up with the Joneses. The real yardstick of our monetary value is net worth.

Write down all your assets, things of value, (car, home, stocks, bonds, etc.) and subtract that amount from all your debts (student loans, credit cards, car loan, mortgage, etc.). Whatever the number, that's your net worth. For example, if I have $10,000 worth of assets (car, retirement account) and $27,000 worth of debts (student loans, car loan, credit cards) then I have a negative net worth of $17,000.

Reader Question
I keep hearing people talk about net worth, but I'm not sure why it is important. Do you know?

Yep. The reason that net worth is so important is it gives you a snap shot of how well you are doing financially. Many of us only think of how much income we bring in and this is a huge mistake, especially in these times.

We have all heard the stories about people that make high six and seven figure incomes having their homes foreclosed, IRS liens imposed, so on and so forth. How are they making so much money, but losing their homes? The reason why these things occur may be that they do not have a snap shot of the bigger picture. It is easy to feel good about your monetary status when you are seeing checks every two weeks, however let's dig a little deeper.

Let's say that person A earns $1,100 every two weeks after taxes. Sounds pretty good right? Well, this person has a beautiful apartment with a rent of $1,100 a month, a car note of $350 a month, and student loan payments of $250 a month. Still doesn't sound too bad, right? We haven't looked at the phone bill, cell phone bill, electricity bill, cable bill, eating out every night and clubbing every weekend expenses.

Every month person A puts a few things on their credit card to cover some of the things that they want to buy. There isn't enough money to buy the things they want, let alone save anything so savings gets put on the back burner. After a year or two of living this way, let's take a look at this person's net worth:

Assets $13,500

Savings $500
401k $3,000
Car value $ 10,000

Liabilities $40,500

Credit card $1, 500
Car loan $12,000
Student loans $27,000

Net worth -$27,000

This person is $27,000 in debt and adding on to it every month by using credit cards to cover their basic needs! We have to stop looking at our incomes as assets. Too many of us are finding out that our jobs are not as secure as we would like. To have a sound idea of what our financial picture looks like we have to start looking at the bigger picture.

Each of us should know our net worth and credit scores off the top of our heads. Hopefully, this explanation has given you a more clear understanding of net worth and how important it is in your life.

Net Worth Worksheet

Assets		
Real estate valuation		
Car(s) valuation		
Investment account totals		
Jewelry		
Total		
Liabilities		
Mortgage balance		
Auto loan balance		
Student loan debt		
Credit card debt		
Debt to family/friends		
Total		

Subtract the liabilities from the assets to find your net worth.

Asset Total $ _____

- minus

Liability Total $ _____

My net worth is $_____

Rapid Refund Loans

Every winter I see signs, online ads, and commercials for rapid refund loans for your tax return. This is a horrible idea. The idea is that you can't wait the 7 days for your money to be deposited electronically into your checking account, for free, or the month it takes for you to receive a check. For the honor of providing you with your money a few days earlier tax refund companies will charge as much as 20%! Instead of thinking about it as getting a bonus, think about it as a repayment of a loan you already made- to the government. Be patient and get all your money back.

Reader Question:

I keep hearing people say that you shouldn't want to get a tax return at the end of the year. Why not?

Good question.

The answer is this: when you pay taxes out of your check every two weeks you are pre-paying for the amount of tax you will owe at the end of the year. When you get a refund, the government is returning the money you *over*paid. That's right. The reason you are getting a nice, fat, refund check is because you gave the government too much of your money during the year.

The best thing to do is try to break even.

Most of us have a pretty constant income. That means that we, generally, know how much we have to pay every year and how much we'll get back at the end of the year. Why wait? I don't know about you, but I need my money now! Instead of waiting until the end of the year why not plan your tax payments accordingly.

You can consult your tax preparer and ask them to run a mock return to find out how much you should be paying every check. Think about it this way: if you knew that you owed your Mom $1,000 and you decided to pay her in installments, would you calculate it so that you paid her $1,000 even or would you calculate it so that you paid her $1,500 and at the end of the year she would give you $500 back?

Sounds rather silly when I put it that way, no?

Plan Ahead

The best advice one can give to help people be financially responsible is this: plan ahead. Plan waaaay ahead. Your bills come every month. Know what day they are due and set aside money to pay bills before they are due. Think of ways that paying early, or in bulk, can reduce your rate. For example, paying your car insurance in one yearly lump sum is usually cheaper than paying every month. Save up ahead of time to pay the yearly rate and save money over the whole year.

Reader Question:

I'd like to answer a question from an event I attended a while ago. We watched the film I.O.U.S.A. (www.I.O.U.S.A.TheMovie.com) and had a lively discussion about the national debt, personal debt, and various other topics. The question that I want to answer is: What should each of us be doing to ensure that we are managing our finances responsibly?

There are 4 very important things that you can do to take responsibility for your financial future:

#1 – Pay your bills on time

Make sure that you know when bills are due and pay before the due date. Some companies take a few days to process the payment, so make sure that your payment is in at least 3 days early if you are paying by check or debit card online, at least 5 days early if you are paying by mail, or before 3pm if you are paying by real time debit card.

#2 – Know your credit score

I have heard people say that, "once you have bad credit, forget it, there's nothing you can do about it". This is wholly incorrect. Your credit score fluctuates every month depending on your on-time payments, debt ratio, length of credit history, etc. Add to the mix that each of the three credit agencies has it's own file for you, and you see why it's not so easy to just say that across the board you have "bad" credit.

#3 – Monitor your credit score

I can not emphasize enough the need to monitor your credit score at each agency. Make sure that the information contained is correct. If you find information that is not correct, log in to each site, write a letter, or call immediately to correct the information. Not only should you worry about you destroying your credit score, you should also be wary of shady companies and identity theft.

#4 – Save for a rainy day

Save at least 15% of your after tax income. That's right, I said it. Do what you have to do to set aside emergency money. Everyone will have unexpected expenses come up, having a stash to pull from could be the difference between beginning a cash advance cycle on your credit cards or at the local check cashing spot and staying financially independent.

Taking care of your financial present can secure your financial future, so think about where you want to be in five years and prepare accordingly.

Check Cashing Places Are the Devil

It seems that I can't watch t.v., drive down the street, or hang out at a hamburger restaurant without seeing an ad for someone's check cashing services or pay day loan or some such craziness. I have read the research, but I still don't understand why so many people don't have checking accounts at credit unions. Even a traditional bank would be better than using check cashing services.

Let me put it this way, paying even $10 to cash your check every two weeks equals $240 a year! Having an account at a credit union or traditional bank enables you to cash your check every pay day with no fee. Pay day loans? These are the worst of the worst. Getting a pay day loan usually starts a cycle that will be hard to get out of. Let's say, you take out a $300 loan until your next pay day. When your check arrives you have to pay your regular bills, plus the $300 loan, plus the loan fee. Most people won't have a spare $300 plus the loan fee. So what happens? You pay the money back and end up needing even more money than you originally borrowed! Please, please, please don't use check cashing companies; open a checking account at a credit union.

Reader Question

My mom has been talking to me about getting a credit union instead of a regular bank. I'm not sure what the difference is or if I should do it. What do you think?

I think it's a great idea! Let me preface this answer by saying that I have been a proud credit union member for about fifteen years. Now, the most significant difference between a bank and a credit union is this: with a credit union you own part of the institution. The Credit Union National Association describes it this way, "credit unions are financial institutions formed by an organized group of people with a common bond. Members of credit unions pool their assets to provide loans and other financial services to each other.". Visit the Credit Union National Association's webpage at http://www.creditunion.coop/) for more information on the differences between credit unions and banks.

The basic difference is this, while banks are trying to make money for their shareholders, credit unions are using the pooled resources of the credit union members to provide loans to all the members of the credit union. Credit unions function very similarly to *njangi* (read an article about the *njangi* at African Vibes Magazine online http://africanvibes.com). Pooling resources is a very good way to get ahead in life. We've all heard that one loc is stronger than one hair, or a might fist is stronger than one finger?

37

The fees for most things at a credit union, including checking and savings account maintenance fees, overdraft fees, and loan rates are lower than at banks. That means that you can save money on those fees. Though the savings may seem small think about how much that $12 account maintenance fee will cost you over ten years. $1,440! Fees are like small leaks in a dam. They start out small and slowly eat away at your money until you can't seem to figure out where your money is going every month.

Deciding to move your money to a credit union is a personal decision that needs to be thought out. Considerations include: where is your closest branch, where is your closest ATM, and what will the new fees be in comparison to your current fees. It might take a little bit of time of research, however it's worth it. Your life is worth it.

To find a local credit union search
http://www.creditunion.coop/cu_locator/quickfind.php.

Save Money on Groceries

We should all be watching our pennies right now so I want to share a few money saving tips:

#1 Look for discounts on groceries by shopping at co-ops. Co-ops are stores that buy in bulk for the members of the co-op only. Co-ops are by the community, for the community. Visit The Coop Directory at http://www.coopdirectory.org for more information.
#2 Create a small window garden to save on herbs and small fruits and veggies. Many fruits, veggies, and herbs can be grown in a small space and taste so much better when grown at home.
#3 Set a food budget and stick to it. We've all heard it before: don't shop when you're hungry, make a list of what you need, and look for sales.
#4 Look for coupons in newspapers, in stores, and online. Sign up for online mailing lists for your favorite foods brands and have coupons delivered to your inbox! Check the weekly newspapers for coupons on items you use frequently, and buy when things are on sale.

Reader Question:

I heard about places that you can buy meat, veggies, etc. from off the farm. What's that about?

It's good that you're thinking about these things. We should all be thinking about where our food comes from and how it's handled before it lands on our dinner plates. What you've heard of is Community Supported Agriculture (find out more at http://www.localharvest.org/csa/).It's a process by which you can pay a farmer for a portion of meat, fruit, and vegetables that you can pick up at designated times during the year, sometimes your food will be delivered to you or your local farmer's market. This is good for two main reasons.

The first good reason is that the food is usually much cheaper. Buying directly from the farm helps keep costs low for the farmer and those savings can be passed on to you. Think about it. You'll get fresh, delicious meat and produce several times a year cheaper than you could get at the grocery store.

The second good reason to go this route is because you're buying local. Buying local helps protect our environment by spending less on fuels to transport the food which also means less pollution in the air. It also may help you figure out where your food is coming from and how it's been grown or raised. In case you haven't heard about

Alimentarius Codex (read more about Alimentarius Codex
http://en.wikipedia.org/wiki/Codex_Alimentarius)there are many people deciding what is and isn't okay for you to consume. You can find a farmer that is organic by Local Harvest at www.LocalHarvest.org Making sure that you are aware of what chemicals, hormones, and pesticides are in your food is an important piece in creating a healthy environment for yourself and your family.

You rock!

If you've made it this far into the book, you have a desire to learn more about personal finance. Hopefully, you've picked up a few tidbits, however there is so much more to do! Take a moment and write down a few next steps that you would like to engage in.

Next Steps Action List

I need to:

To do that, I need to gather this information:

I will have this step completed by:

I need to:

To do that, I need to gather this information:

I will have this step completed by:

www.ingramcontent.com/pod-product-compliance
Lightning Source LLC
Chambersburg PA
CBHW081230170526
45165CB00009B/3025